Always Two Sides Series

Kelsey and the New Girl in School

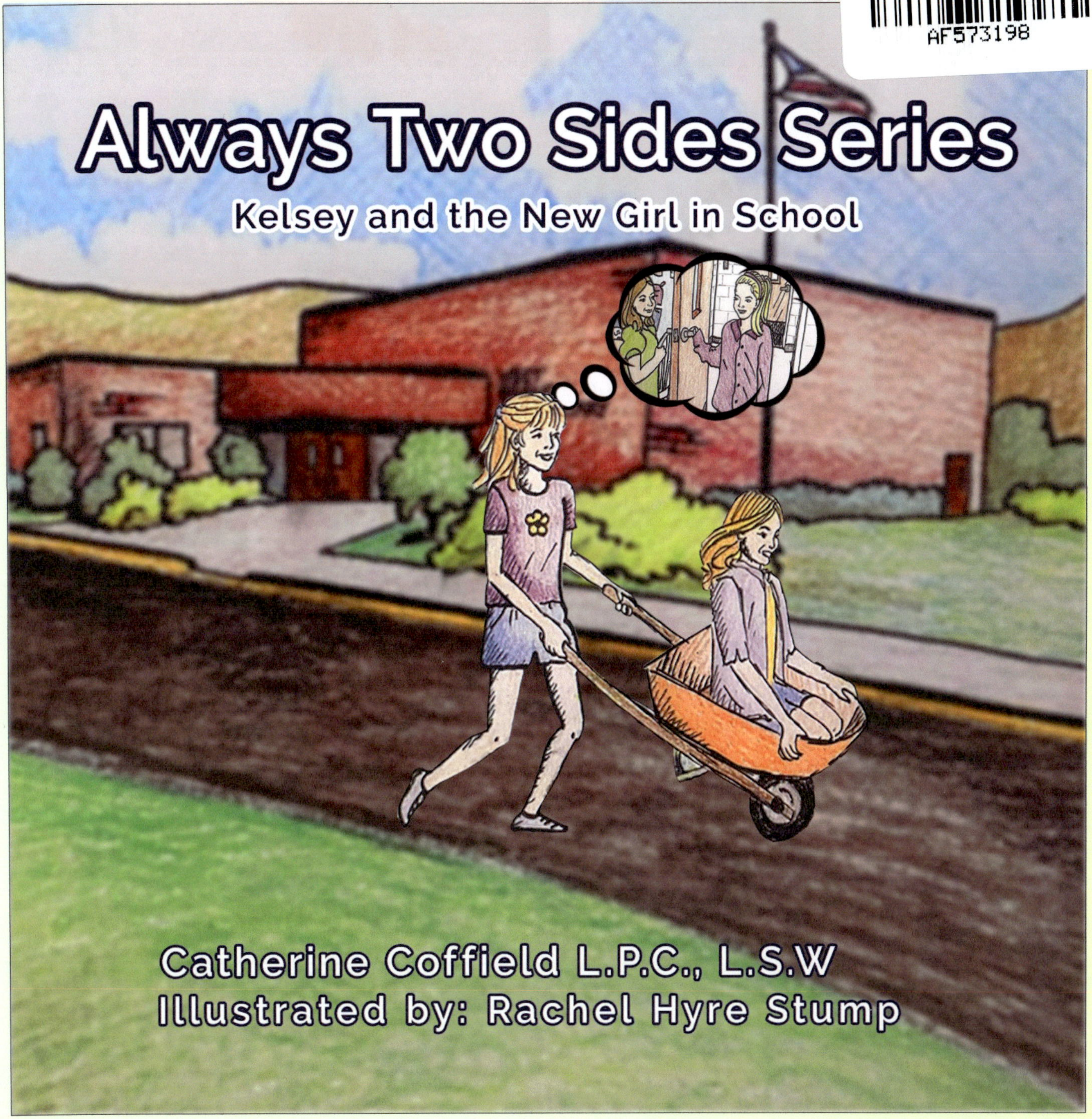

Catherine Coffield L.P.C., L.S.W
Illustrated by: Rachel Hyre Stump

Always Two Sides Series

Kelsey and the New Girl in School

Published in the United States of America

ISBN 979-8-89395-845-4 (SC)
ISBN 979-8-89395-844-7 (Ebook)

Library of Congress Control Number: 2024921992

Coffield Publishing
944 Lakeview Dr Horner,
WV 26372, USA
catherineann13@gmail.com

Order Information and Rights Permission:

Quantity sales. Special discounts might be available on quantity purchases by corporations, associations, and others. For details, contact the publisher at the address above.

For Book Rights Adaptation and other Rights Permission.
Call us at toll-free 1-888-945-8513 or send us an email at admin@stellarliterary.com.

"KELSEY AND THE NEW GIRL IN SCHOOL"

ALWAYS TWO SIDES
A NEW GIRL IN SCHOOL

STORY ONE:
THROUGH KELSEY'S EYES

Hi. My name is Kelsey and my best friend is Anna. We've been friends since preschool. Now we're third graders at West Branch Elementary in Sunny Buck, West Virginia.

Anna and I have sooo many awesome memories. We built a really cool club house in Anna's backyard. We buried a friendship box filled with letters and other things that represent our friendship.

There was this time when we took turns pushing each other around in my grandpa's wheelbarrow. We had a TOTAL blast!

Every day after school we do our homework together and play until Anna's mom gets home from work. Sometimes we make chocolate chip cookies with my mom. We both love dunking our cookies in milk.

On the bus, Anna and I always sit together. We talk about the funniest and weirdest things. We have so much fun... all the time.

Our favorite things on the playground at recess are four-square, hop-scotch, and of course, swinging. When our teacher, Mrs. Phillips, assigns projects with partners, we always pick each other.

Everything was wonderful. Then suddenly, things seemed to change. Lately, we've had some problems. Have you been friends with someone but then things start to go wrong and you just aren't sure what to do?

About three weeks ago, a new girl came to our school. Her name is Kirsten. Mrs. Phillips sat Kirsten next to me and asked me to show her around and help her feel more comfortable at school. At first, everything was great. Kirsten was nice and interesting. I showed her all around and introduced her to students and teachers.

She ate with Anna and me at lunch, and sat right behind us on our bus. We all played together at recess. We were all getting along really well, but then I started to feel left out. One night I called Anna. She said she was on the other line with Kirsten and that she'd call me right back. She never called me back. I felt soooo sad.

The next morning when I got on the bus, Kirsten was in MY seat next to Anna. I had to sit behind them. I felt jealous. Anna turned around to talk to me a couple of times, but it just didn't feel the same.

In class, we were getting ready to work on a project with partners. Kirsten immediately asked Anna, "Will you be my partner?"

"SURE!" Anna answered excitedly. Then she turned toward me with a worried look on her face. She said, "I hope you don't mind if I am partners with Kirsten this time. We can take turns. I'll be your partner next time."

What could I say? Sadly, I said, "Okay" and I paired up with Laura.

At lunchtime, they didn't even save me a seat. I felt really angry. I yelled at Anna, "You make me sooo mad! You aren't my friend anymore and I wish Kirsten never came to our school!" After all, I was the person who introduced them to each other and invited Kirsten into our friendship!

I had enough! This just wasn't fair. Still, I didn't like the feelings I had inside after shouting at Anna. I wasn't quite sure what to do. Then I remembered that our school counselor, Mrs. Coffield, had helped my older brother, Brandin, when he was in the fourth grade. I needed some help with this, so I went to see Mrs. Coffield.

I felt a little nervous at first. She smiled and asked, "What can I help you with today, Miss Kelsey?"

I felt kind of embarrassed, and it was hard to talk about what was going on inside of me. I wasn't really sure how to put it all into words. After a while, I just blurted it out. "Anna and I've been friends for sooo long, and we're always together. Now, there is this new girl in school who is driving me bonkers. Anna is hanging out with her more than me. Today, she even picked her for her partner. I don't know what to do. What can I do?"

Mrs. Coffield and I talked about everything that was bothering me. I learned that other kids had similar problems. I guess kids are really a lot more alike than different. Talking to Mrs. Coffield helped me feel a lot better. I realize friendships change as we get older and even though I don't like it, there are some things I can do to feel better about the situation.

Here's what I did. That night, I wrote in my journal the things I would like to say to Anna. I wanted to apologize but also wanted to let her know how I was really feeling. Mrs. Coffield suggested starting my sentences with "I feel" or "I wish" when talking with Anna about things. Anna would be more likely to listen to what I was saying if she didn't feel I was attacking her with my words.

That next day at school,
I apologized to Anna and explained to her how I felt left out and scared of the changes happening in our friendship. She gave me a BIG hug.

We both agreed we'd try harder to keep our friendship strong.

I've been getting to know Laura better, too. When Anna and Kirsten are hanging out, instead of getting upset, I have someone else who's really fun to pal around with. Laura and I like the same cartoons and we both have aquariums with colorful fish. She's also very funny and makes me laugh.

I feel much better now, and even though it's not always easy to accept these changes, I've come to realize Kirsten is really funny and there are some really neat things about her. She's really good in math and helps me with my homework while we're waiting for the bus to arrive at the end of the day.

Now I have three REALLY good friends-Anna, Laura, and Kirsten. Sometimes we all hang out together. Last weekend we had a slumber party at my house. Lying in a circle on my living room floor, we ate popcorn, told funny stories, and laughed until we cried! We were having so much fun, my older sister Briana even joined in our fun.

Making and keeping friends takes some work. Do you have ideas on how to keep friendships strong?

"KIRSTEN, THE NEW GIRL IN SCHOOL"

ALWAYS TWO SIDES
A NEW GIRL IN SCHOOL

STORY TWO:
THROUGH KIRSTEN'S EYES

Hi, I'm Kirsten. I just moved to a small town called Sunny Buck in the rolling hills of West Virginia. It is totally different than the flat, big city of Dallas, Texas, where I used to live. I didn't want to move here, but my dad was transferred here with his job.

Have you ever been a new student in a school? Starting a new school is really hard. I really miss all of my friends in Texas. On that first day at West Branch Elementary School, I could feel my palms sweating and it seemed like there were knots in my tummy.

I sat in the office while my mom filled out some paperwork. I watched lots of other kids go by. They were talking and laughing. I wondered, *Will I ever have a friend to talk and laugh with again? What if nobody likes me? What if my teacher is mean?*

Finally, Dr. Stankus, the school principal, walked me to my classroom. She introduced me to my new teacher, Mrs. Phillips. Mrs. Phillips seemed very kind as she smiled and welcomed me to the class. Mrs. Phillips sat me next to a girl named Kelsey and asked her to show me around the school. I liked Kelsey. She knew everybody and was very helpful. She showed me the lunch room, art room, music room, and the counselor's office.

Kelsey shared her books with me until I received my own set. Kelsey introduced me to her friend, Anna. Anna treated me as if she had known me all her life. It didn't take me long to see that Anna was really funny and kind to everyone.

Anna and Kelsey seemed very close. They told each other *everything*. Sometimes I felt weird when they talked about things, I had no idea about. I wondered if I'd ever truly fit in.

On the school bus, I sat in back of Kelsey and Anna. One day Anna fell out of her seat on the bus. We all laughed until we cried. We hung out during recess and lunch, too. Anna and Kelsey loved to play four-square. I had no idea what it was at first. I was nervous about trying it, but once I did, it was totally fun.

Anna phoned me every day after school. One day she asked me to sit with her on the bus. I was worried Kelsey would get mad, but Anna said, "Kelsey is great! She won't mind at all." But, when Kelsey saw me in her seat, she had a hurt look on her face. I asked her if she wanted her seat back, but she just shook her head no and sat quietly in the seat behind us. I was worried she was upset.

Anna and I started to spend more and more time together. Kelsey started to act differently toward me. I felt like she didn't want me to hang around with her and Anna. I was feeling sad and confused.

At lunch one day, Kelsey yelled at me and Anna. She said, "I wish you never came to our school." That really hurt my feelings. I'm not exactly sure what I'd done. I thought we were all friends. I started to worry about being the new girl in school. I was afraid Kelsey might get the entire school mad at me.

I talked to my mom about it. She suggested I talk to our school counselor to see if she could help me figure out my problem. Our school counselor's name is Mrs. Coffield. When she comes to the classroom, she seems really nice and very cool. She talks to us about being kind to each other and other things. I had met her my very first day of school. She said she likes to personally welcome every new student to our school. I heard from other kids that she was great to talk to when you have a problem. I had a serious problem, so I decided to give her a try.

Mrs. Coffield kept a lot of neat things in her room. I decided to play in the little sand box on her table. This helped me to relax and made it much easier for me to tell her what I was thinking. The other kids were right. She's great to talk to! She helped me come up with some ideas to make my troubles better.

I knew it wouldn't be easy, but I decided to try some of the things that we talked about. First, I talked to Kelsey about how I felt and how much I'd like for us to be friends. I wrote my thoughts down first, so the words would come out the way I wanted them too. I offered to help her with her math homework and she offered to help me with science.

I made it a point to talk to Kelsey more. After some time went by, we even agreed to take turns sitting together on the bus. Sometimes I got to sit with Kelsey and other times with Anna. When it was their turn to sit together, I sat with another neat girl, Laura, who was one of Kelsey's other friends. Laura's really interesting. She has fish and named one of them Kirsten!

Sometimes I feel a little jealous over how close Kelsey and Anna are. It really makes me miss my best friend, Callie, back in Texas.

If I start to feel upset with Kelsey, I remember that first day of school at West Branch and how she helped me feel accepted and more comfortable.

I realize it's great to have both Anna and Kelsey as friends. I've even been hanging out with Laura, too. It's really fun when all four of us do things together. At recess, we swing and play four-square. Often, we play in Anna's clubhouse in her backyard. Anna's mom even takes us all to the mall sometimes.

Last weekend, I went to Kelsey's house for a sleepover. At first, I felt a little nervous. But, it didn't take me long to loosen up. We all danced around her living room and sang songs. We ate popcorn while we laid on the floor talking about girl stuff. We were laughing so hard, even Kelsey's big sister, Briana, joined in on our fun.

Making and keeping friends takes some effort. Do you have some ideas about keeping friendships strong?